A Hat Full of Jokes and Riddles

by
Chris Tait

Copyright © 2003 Kidsbooks, Inc.
230 Fifth Avenue
New York, NY 10001

Manufactured in the United States of America

0703-1K

Visit us at **www.kidsbooks.com**

Contents

Hilarious Hat Jokes

What do a hockey player and a
magician have in common?

Hat tricks!

Sally: Whenever I'm down in the dumps,
I buy myself a new hat.
Callie: Oh, so that's where you get them!

What did the hat say to the hat rack?

"You hang out here, and I'll go on a-head!"

Why did the Pilgrims have a hard time keeping their pants up?

Because they wore their belt buckles on their hats!

What do you call a dinosaur that wears a cowboy hat?

Tyrannosaurus tex!

What fish wears a cowboy hat?

Billy the Squid!

If you drop a yellow hat in the Red Sea, what does it become?

Wet!

A man was walking in the rain with no umbrella and no hat, but his hair did not get wet. How?

He was bald!

6

What happened to the witch with the crooked nose?

Every time she sneezed, her hat blew off!

Why didn't the woman trust her wide-brimmed hat?

There was just something shady about it!

What did the engineer think about her useful hat?

She thought that it was very cap-able!

A woman and her son went out to the beach for the day to watch the waves roll in. When they arrived, the boy jumped up on a rock to get a better view.

Suddenly, a giant wave rolled in and swept him away.

The woman got down on her knees and said, "Please, please return my son to me!"

Suddenly, a second wave rushed up and dumped the boy back down on the beach. The woman checked him over carefully and then yelled up at the sky, "Hey, when we got here, he had a hat on!"

How is your hat like a bowl of soup?

You fill it to the brim!

Why did the smart man wear a hefty hat?

So he would have something heavy on his mind!

What rider never needs a hat?

The headless horseman!

Why did the witch poke the warlock with her hat?

So that he would get the point!

What kind of hat spins the best?

A top hat!

**What do you call a hat
that a rabbit wears?**

A hop hat!

Why are hats always hungry?

*Because they always have to be
off during dinner!*

**Why did the construction
worker dislike his cap?**

Because it was a hard hat to get along with!

What kind of headwear do horses love best?

Straw hats!

Why did the man think his rain hat was so cool?

Because it made him feel slicker!

What did the hat say to the side of the head?

"Ears looking at you!"

Animal Antics

What is the most up-to-date animal in the zoo?

The gnu!

How much is a skunk worth?

One scent!

What kind of book is *Black Beauty*?

A pony-tail!

Farmer #1: Why does your son cluck like a chicken?

Farmer #2: Because he thinks he's a chicken.

Farmer #1: Why don't you tell him he's not a chicken?

Farmer #2: Because we need the eggs!

What kind of shoes do frogs wear on vacation?

Open-toad sandals!

Of all the big cats, which one do you know you can never trust?

The cheetah!

What feathered creature is the most sarcastic of all flying beasts?

The mockingbird!

What do you call a bear with no shoes?

Bear-foot!

Which animal in the zoo is always sick to its stomach?

The yak!

Why did the pig have ink all over its face?

Because it just came out of the pen!

Why did the elephant walk on two feet?

To give the ants a chance!

Where is the one place a dog won't shop?

A flea market!

Zookeeper #1: I've lost one of my elephants!
Zookeeper #2: Why don't you put an ad
in the paper?
Zookeeper #1: Don't be silly! It can't read!

Why was Billy so mad?

Because somebody got his goat!

Why don't snakes use utensils?

Because they have forked tongues!

A team of little animals and a team of big animals decided to play a game of football against each other.

During the first half of the game, the big animals were winning. But during the second half of the game, the little animals started to catch up. They won, thanks to a centipede that scored every touchdown.

When the game was over, the chipmunk asked the centipede, "Where were you during the first half of the game?"

The centipede looked at the chipmunk and said, "Putting on my shoes!"

Why do tigers eat raw meat?

Because they're bad cooks!

Why did the snake go to the doctor?

Because it was feeling low!

Who do you get to make your calls in the swamp?

The croc-o-dial!

What do you call a sleeping bull?

A bulldozer!

What animal is no fun at a party?

A boar!

Why are fish easier to weigh than humans?

Because they come with their own scales!

Marvelous Magic Jokes

How did the magician know that his assistant was in pieces?

Because he saw her!

What was the injured magician wearing?

A cast, of course!

Are there any sorcerer athletes?

Yes, Magic Johnson!

**How would you describe a joke about
a rabbit being pulled out of a hat?**

Very bunny!

**What do you call a magician who
can't stand still?**

A magic wand-erer!

What did the magician say after he fell on stage?

"And now, for my next trip . . ."

What did the magician call her trick of getting out of the sewer?

The grate escape!

A magician wanted to try out a new trick. He asked his assistant to help. "Please get in this box," he said. "I would like to try sawing you."

She thought about it, then told him that she would try it. She got in the box and he sawed away. After a while, she asked him, "Well, did it work?"

"I don't know," he said. "I'll half to go see!"

What did the magician say to the chicken?

"Peck a card, any card!"

**What did the magician say before
she drove away?**

"Abra car-dabra!"

What do you call a magician with little fingers?

Slight of hand!

What did the magician say about his hat-and-rabbit trick?

That it was a hare-raising routine!

What do you call a trickster with a pole?

A fishin' magician!

What did the magician name his daughter?

Wand-a!

What did everyone call the phony magician?

The magic-sham!

What do you call a polite hypnotist?

Charming!

What did the magician think about magic school?

It wizarder [was harder] than he thought!

What did the magician say when he made the pig disappear?

"The ham is faster than the eye!"

What do you call tricks performed in the dark?

Black magic!

What do you call a wizard on the beach?

A magic-tan!

What did the assistant call the magician's rope trick?

Knotty!

Why did the magician's rope trick fail?

He forgot to wear his tie!

★ ☾ ★

What do you call a cool magician?

A hip-notist!

What do magicians call their winter show?

The cold spell!

How do magicians learn so fast?

With hocus focus!

What did the magician say to pull the feline out of the hat?

"Abra cat-abra!"

How can a magician enrich your mind?

*When she pulls a quarter out
of your ear!*

**What did the magician's housekeeper
take care of?**

The magic dust, of course!

Why do magicians have such big shirts?

Because they always have something up their sleeves!

What would you play in a magician's band?

The magic flute!

Ridiculous Riddles

What goes up but never goes down?

Your age!

If an electric train was going south, which way would the steam blow?

Nowhere, because electric trains don't have steam!

How could a cowboy ride into town on Friday,
stay two days, and ride out on Friday?

Because his horse was named Friday!

What becomes smaller when you
add two letters to it?

Small!

What is so fragile that just saying its name can break it?

Silence!

Why can't bikes stand up by themselves?

Because they are too tired (two-tired)!

What can go up a chimney down, but won't go down a chimney up?

An umbrella!

What 11-letter English word is always pronounced incorrectly?

Incorrectly!

There is a recipe that says, "Throw out the outside. Cook the inside. Eat the outside. Throw out the inside." What is this recipe for?

Corn on the cob!

What gets wet while it dries?

A towel!

What can run but not walk?

Water!

When can bad grades get you all wet?

When they are below C level!

What runs but never walks, has a mouth but never talks, and has a bed but never sleeps?

A river!

A football team was getting ready to play in
the finals. Just before the game, the coach
had to go to the bank. Why?

To get his quarter back!

What has no lungs but needs air, is not alive
but grows, and makes noise but has no mouth?

A fire!

Silly School Jokes

What did the student say when the teacher asked him to pay a little attention?

"I'm paying as little as I can!"

Teacher: Kathy, what is the most popular answer to a teacher's question?
Kathy: I don't know.
Teacher: That's correct!

A man escaped from jail by digging a hole from his cell to the outside world. When his work was finally done, he came out of his tunnel in the middle of a school playground.

"I'm free, I'm free!" he shouted.

"So what?" said a little girl who was riding her tricycle. "I'm four!"

How did the teacher know that the student's father had not helped her with her homework?

All the answers were wrong!

Why did the teacher want to teach at a country school after working in the city?

He heard that the population was less dense in the country!

What does a teacher call doing your homework?

Detention prevention!

Teacher: Even a six-year-old could answer that question!
Student: No wonder I don't know it—I'm ten!

Why did the teacher have to tell his student that she was failing math?

Because the student wasn't so good with numbers!

Teacher: You haven't made anything all day!
Student: I've made a lot of mistakes. Don't
they count?

Nicole: Today my teacher yelled at me for
something that I didn't do.
Amelia: What was that?
Nicole: My homework!

Student: I don't deserve a zero on this test!
Teacher: I agree, but there is nothing less
I can give you!

What kind of teachers wear sunglasses?

The ones with bright students!

Why did the boy take a top hat and cape to his exam?

He was hoping to use math-magics!

What did the boy say when he was told that he forgot everything he learned?

"Can you repeat the question?"

Rodney and Bruce were best friends. One day, they were at a school carnival. Rodney went on the ferris wheel. After a few minutes, there was an accident and the wheel went crashing down to the ground. Bruce dashed over to a dazed Rodney and asked, "Are you hurt, Rodney?"

"Yes, I am," said Rodney. "I went around three times and you didn't wave once!"

Why wasn't the English teacher good at geometry?

Because she came at it from the wrong angle!

How did the spelling teacher spell relief?

S-U-M-M-E-R!

What did the student say when the math teacher asked him what he would have if he got $20 from 10 people?

"A new skateboard!"

Nifty Knock-Knocks

Knock, knock!
Who's there?
Abra!
Abra who?
Abracadabra!

Knock, knock!
Who's there?
Penny!
Penny who?
Penny for your thoughts!

Knock, knock!
Who's there?
Madge!
Madge who?
Madgical!

Knock, knock!
Who's there?
Copperfield!
Copperfield who?
Copperfield sick, so I came instead!

Knock, knock!
Who's there?
Agatha!
Agatha who?
Agatha sore tooth! It's killing me!

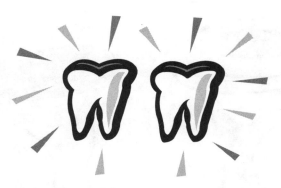

Knock, knock!
Who's there?
Ollie!
Ollie who?
Ollie want for Christmas is my two front teeth!

Knock, knock!
Who's there?
Harry!
Harry who?
Harry up and take me to the dentist!

Knock, knock!
Who's there?
Mission!
Mission who?
Missin' you, that's who!

Knock, knock!
Who's there?
Super!
Super who?
Soup or sandwich?

Knock, knock!
Who's there?
Mucky!
Mucky who?
Muh key is stuck!

Knock, knock!
Who's there?
Suture!
Suture who?
Suit yourself, don't let me in!

Knock, knock!
Who's there?
Briefcase!
Briefcase who?
Brief case of amnesia. Give me a minute!

HELLO?

Knock, knock!
Who's there?
Headphone!
Headphone who?
Had phoned ahead, but no one answered!

Knock, knock!
Who's there?
Izmi!
Izmi who?
Is me! I just told you!

Knock, knock!
Who's there?
Benny!
Benny who?
Benny where interesting lately?

Knock, knock!
Who's there?
Pepper!
Pepper who?
Pepperoni pizza, that's who!

Knock, knock!
Who's there?
Disappoint!
Disappoint who?
Dis da point where you remember who I am!

Knock, knock!
Who's there?
Bunny!
Bunny who?
Bunny you should ask!

Knock, knock!
Who's there?
Planet!
Planet who?
Plan it early and you'll be fine!

Knock, knock!
Who's there?
Curtain!
Curtain who?
Kurt and me both want to come in!

Knock, knock!
Who's there?
Toenail!
Toenail who?
Tony'll be along in a minute!

Knock, knock!
Who's there?
Gnome!
Gnome who?
Gnome is where the heart is!

Knock, knock!
Who's there?
Keystone!
Keystone who?
Keys don't work. Open up!

Knock, knock!
Who's there?
Opener!
Opener who?
Open 'er up and let me in!

Knock, knock!
Who's there?
Walleye!
Walleye who?
Well, I will tell you when you open up!

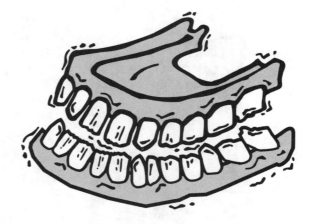

Knock, knock!
Who's there?
Matisse!
Matisse who?
Ma teeth are chattering, I'm freezing!

Knock, knock!
Who's there?
Yosemite!
Yosemite who?
Yo, Sam it is me!

Knock, knock!
Who's there?
Fuller!
Fuller who?
Full of yourself, aren't you?

Knock, knock!
Who's there?
Sunday!
Sunday who?
Sun day you'll remember my name!

Knock, knock!
Who's there?
Police!
Police who?
Police let me in, I need to use the bathroom!

Knock, knock!
Who's there?
Yucan!
Yucan who?
You can lead a horse to water,
but you can't make it drink!

Pet Punch Lines

What did the cat say after it chased and caught the rat?

"Sorry, my mousestake!"

What do you get when you cross a cat with a fish?

A purr-ahna!

What pet always has a sore throat?

A horse [hoarse]!

What kind of dogs always get into fights?

Boxers!

Which side of a dog has the most hair?

The outside!

What soda does a pet frog like the best?

Cherry croak!

Why should you never tell secrets to a pet pig?

Because it is bound to squeal!

How do you write to your pet hog?

With a pigpen!

What did one cat say to the other cat after it saw that they were being followed by a dog?

"Don't look now, but I think we're being tailed!"

What do you say to your horse if it looks unhappy?

"What's with the long face?"

When should you take your pet chicks to the vet?

When it's time for their rooster shots!

How can a pet salamander spend all day in the rain and not get a single hair wet?

Because salamanders don't have hair!

What kind of bird gulps the loudest?

The swallow!

Why did the little old lady want to get rid of her pet bird?

Because it used fowl language!

What do you say when you want to talk with your pet python?

"Let's get together and wrap!"

Why don't flying mice make good pets?

Bats me!

Cross-the-Road Crack-Ups

Why did the chicken cross the road?

To get to the other side!

Why did the starfish cross the road?

To get to the other tide!

Why did the fox cross the road?

To get the chicken!

Why did the piece of gum cross the road?

It was stuck to the chicken's foot!

Why did the pigs cross the road?

To do their hogwash!

Why did the turkey cross the road twice?

To prove it was not a chicken!

Why did the weasel cross the road twice?

Because he was a double-crosser!

Why didn't the skeleton cross the road?

Because it didn't have the guts!

**Why did the chicken go halfway
across the road?**

To lay it on the line!

Why did the dog cross the road?

To get out of the barking lot!

Why did the cat cross the road?

It just wanted to have a purr-pose!

Why did the kid cross the road?

To get to the other slide!

Why did the apple cross the road?

To get saucy!

Why did the orange cross the road?

It juice felt like it!

Why did the bee cross the road?

Someone told it to buzz off!

Why did the butterfly cross the road?

It was in a flap about something!

Why did the cow cross the road?

It was just moo-ved to do it!

Why did the bunch of grapes cross the road?

They wanted to cross the wine!

**Why did the rabbit cross the road
with a calculator?**

*Because it heard someone say
it should multiply!*

Why did the pumpkin cross the road?

It wanted to play squash!

Why did the puppy cross the road?

To pick up its litter!

Why did the zebra cross the road?

To show its stripes!

Why did the horse cross the road?

To visit its fodder!

Why did the tomatoes cross the road?

They just wanted to ketchup!

Why did the goose cross the road?

To get some eggs-ercise!

Why did the chameleon cross the road?

It just wanted a change of scene!

Why did the banana cross the road?

It just slipped up!

Why did the chair cross the road?

To seat the sights!

How did the deck of cards cross the road?

It just shuffled over!

Why did the spaghetti cross the road?

It didn't want to get stranded!

Why did the fish cross the road?

They were on a school trip!

Why did the hat cross the road?

To get a-head!

Why did the spoon cross the road?

To get to the fork in it!

Why did the elf cross the road?

To take a short-cut!

Why did the egg cross the road?

It wanted to get crackin'!

Why did the elephant run across the road?

To jog its memory!

Food Funnies

What kind of soup is fresh in the cafeteria, but still boring?

Chicken new-dull!

What makes a cook sadder the skinnier it gets?

An onion!

Why did the cook take a job making bread for the cafeteria?

Because he kneaded the dough!

How did the cup and the saucer feel about the quick way they had been washed?

They thought it was dish-picable!

What did the female mushroom say about the male mushroom?

"He's a real fun guy (fungi)!"

Stan: I trained my dog not to beg at the table.
Fran: How did you do that?
Stan: I let it taste my cooking.

How did the cheese feel after it was shredded?

It was grate-ful!

What does a tree like to drink with lunch?

Root beer!

What is golden soup made of?

Fourteen carrots!

What did the French student say after eating lunch at the cafeteria?

"Mercy [merci]!"

Two friends were standing in line at a fast-food restaurant, waiting to place their orders. There was a big sign posted by the register that read, "No bills larger than $20 accepted." One friend said to the other, "Believe me, if I *had* a bill larger than $20, I wouldn't be eating here!"

Why should you go to the cafeteria before computer class?

To grab a little byte!

Diner: Waiter, why have you given me my dinner in a feed bag?
Waiter: Because the cook says that you eat like a horse!

Diner: Waiter, your tie is in my soup!
Waiter: That's all right, sir. It's not shrinkable.

Diner: Waiter, your thumb is in my soup!
Waiter: That's all right, miss. The soup isn't hot.

Diner: Waiter, what is this in my soup?
Waiter: I'm not sure, sir. I can't tell one bug from another!

**Why did the student start a food fight
with her meatloaf?**

The only other option was to eat it!

**When there is only one thing on the menu
at school, how can you still have a choice
of what to eat?**

You can choose not to eat it!

**What do you say when you find a dead bug
in your soup at school?**

"It must have tasted it!"

What do you call baked goods prepared by the Seven Dwarfs?

Short-bread!

What is the heaviest kind of food?

Pound cake!

What do you get from cows after an earthquake?

Milkshakes!

How can you sing underwater?

With a tune-a-fish!

**How can you share five apples
with ten friends?**

Make apple pie!

What do the magic sisters eat at the beach?

Sand-witches!

What is the vampire's least favorite food?

Garlic stake [steak]!

What is the one thing you should take before every meal?

A seat!

Why are piñatas never hungry?

Because they are always stuffed!

What food do you give your cat for dessert on Valentine's Day?

Chocolate mouse, of course!

Why should you never eat the comics that come with your gum?

Because they taste funny!

When is the best day to eat eggs?

Fry-day!

What color is a belch?

Burple!

What kind of vegetable is named after its own recipe?

Squash!

When is violence allowed in the kitchen?

When you are beating eggs!

How can you be mean to milk?

When you are whipping cream!

Why did the baker tease the bread?

To see if he could get a rise out of it!

What did the chef say about her first book?

"It's baste on a true story!"

What kind of ring makes a jeweler cry?

An onion ring!

What is the most unhappy fruit?

Crab apples!

Why do newspaper writers eat only from the middle of the ice cream?

Because they want the inside scoop!

What do witches like in their coffee?

Scream and sugar!

EEEEK!

Just for Laughs

What do you call the key to an ape's cage?

A mon-key!

Who are the smartest insects?

Spelling bees!

HAT

What did the llama say when it read the paper?

"Hey, that's gnus to me!"

How do you describe a shy vampire?

Bats-ful!

What do you call a knight with no home?

A bedless horseman!

What do astronomers sing in the bath?

"When You Wash Upon a Star!"

How do cats stop their favorite videos?

They put them on paws!

What do trolls call their after-school assignments?

Gnome work!

Where do down-on-their-luck fish end up?

On squid row!

Where did Sir Lancelot go to pick up his high school diploma?

Knight school!

What do you say when you want knights to stop fighting?

"Wait joust a moment!"

What do housekeeper rodents do?

Mousework!

What is the most interesting thing about the word *knight*?

It has a duel meaning!

When is it difficult to take three teaspoons of medicine every day?

When you have only two teaspoons!

How many seconds are in a year?

Twelve, starting with the second of January!

Two similar snakes were slithering down the road. One snake turned to the other and asked, "Are we poisonous?"
"Why?" the other snake asked.
"Because I just bit my lip!"